LIFE TRANSFORMATION DAY BY DAY

A 31-DAY DEVOTIONAL

DEBORA BARR

All scripture quotations, unless otherwise indicated, are taken from the New King James Version®. Copyright © 1982 by Thomas Nelson, Inc. Used by permission. All rights reserved. Scripture quotations marked NIV are taken from the HOLY BIBLE, NEW INTERNATIONAL VERSION ® Copyright © 1973, 1978, 1984 Biblica. Used by permission of Zondervan. All rights reserved. Scripture quotations marked KJV are taken from the King James Version. Public domain.

Life Transformation Day by Day
A 31-Day Devotional

ISBN: 978-1-948794-26-8 (paperback)
ISBN: 978-1-948794-27-5 (eBook)

Library of Congress Control Number: 2018957891

Printed in the United States of America.

Copyright © 2018 by Debora Barr
DBarrMinistries@gmail.com
www.allthingsnewlifetransformation.org

True Potential, Inc.
PO Box 904
Travelers Rest, SC 29690
www.truepotentialmedia.com

No part of this book may be reproduced or transmitted in any form or by any means, electronic or mechanical, including photocopying, recording or by any information storage and retrieval system, without permission in writing from the publisher.

Contents

Preface 5
Day 1 God's Word is Life-Giving 7
Day 2 God's Love 13
Day 3 Freedom in Truth 18
Day 4 Hearing God's Voice 23
Day 5 Communicating with God 28
Day 6 Understanding the Root Causes of Sin 33
Day 7 Salvation 38
Day 8 Forgiving Others 43
Day 9 Forgiving Ourselves 48
Day 10 Key to Life is Death to Self 53
Day 11 Walking in Integrity 58
Day 12 Spiritual Warfare 64
Day 13 The Heart 70
Day 14 My Hiding Place 75
Day 15 Our Authority in Christ 80
Day 16 Removing Hindrances to Effective Prayer 85
Day 17 Holy Spirit's Power for Inner Healing 90
Day 18 Listening Prayer for Personal Healing 96
Day 19 Power of Sharing Your Testimony 101

Day 20 Exposing Pain and Glorifying God	106
Day 21 In All Things Praise the Lord	111
Day 22 Sharing What God has Done for You with Others	116
Day 23 Witnessing: The Great Commission	122
Day 24 What is Faith?	127
Day 25 Trust in the Lord	132
Day 26 Fear of the Lord	137
Day 27 Abiding in Christ	142
Day 28 Sanctification: A Life-Long Process	147
Day 29 Spiritual Gifts and Calling	152
Day 30 Your Life's Purpose	157
Day 31 Continuing Intimacy with Jesus	163
About the Author	168

Preface

The Bible is not just an ancient history book. It contains the very words of God that we desperately need to hear today. It reveals God's plan from the beginning of time to restore sinful humanity to Him through the sinless life, substitutionary death, and bodily resurrection of Jesus Christ. The Scriptures also bring us comfort and correction,

> *"For the word of God is living and powerful,*
> *and sharper than any two-edged sword,*
> *piercing even to the division of soul and spirit,*
> *and of joints and marrow, and is a discerner*
> *of the thoughts and intents of the heart."*
>
> (Hebrews 4:12).

When I first surrendered my life to Jesus Christ, I began reading the Bible every day to learn more about this God who pursued me with His love when I was living in open rebellion to Him. I not only read the Bible, but I began to apply the Word to my life and was astonished again and again, as I experienced transformation in so many areas of my life. At one point, I shared with my pastor that I felt like my DNA had changed.

I encourage you to participate in this 31-day devotional with a friend or prayer partner. Talk about the daily devotion and your answers to the questions at the end of each topic to receive even greater insight into what God is communicating to you that day. After you complete all 31 lessons, I challenge you to start over at the beginning of this book and slowly repeat the lessons. This time feel free to take more than a day to meditate on each devotion as you interact with the Scriptures and with God through prayer.

Life transformation is possible for you!

> *Therefore, if anyone is in Christ, he is a new creation; old things have passed away; behold, all things have become new.*
>
> (2 Corinthians 5:17)

Day 1

God's Word is Life-Giving

But his delight is in the law of the Lord,
And in His law he meditates day and night.
He shall be like a tree
Planted by the rivers of water,
That brings forth its fruit in its season,
Whose leaf also shall not wither;
And whatever he does shall prosper.

Psalm 1:2–3

God speaks to us today through his written Word, which has the amazing power to transform your life if you read and study it daily. In fact, the Bible is the best-selling book of all time and has stood the test of time. It was written by more than 40 men over approximately 1,300 years from about 1000 BC to 100 AD. It is full of stories about real people who will make you think about your own life, teach you life lessons, encourage you, and sometimes correct your thinking.

It is living and powerful and discerns the thoughts and intents of our hearts (Hebrews 4:12–13). It is inspired by God and equips us for the work God has for our lives (2 Timothy 3:16–17). There are numerous Scriptures in the Bible in which God tells us about the power of His Word to transform our lives:

Joshua 1:8 — *This Book of the Law shall not depart from your mouth, but you shall meditate in it day and night, that you may observe to do according to all that is written in it. For then you will make your way prosperous, and then you will have good success.*

Jeremiah 23:29 — *"Is not My word like a fire?" says the Lord, "And like a hammer that breaks the rock in pieces?"*

1 Peter 1:23 — *…the word of God … lives and abides forever.*

1 Thessalonians 2:13 — *For this reason we also thank God without ceasing, because when you received the word of God which you heard from us, you welcomed it not as the word of men, but as it is in truth, the word of God, which also effectively works in you who believe.*

John 17:17 — *Sanctify them by Your truth. Your word is truth.*

Acts 20:32 — *So now, brethren, I commend you to God and to the word of His grace, which is able to build you up and give you an inheritance among all those who are sanctified.*

God's Word makes us prosperous and successful. It breaks up sin in our lives, lives and abides forever, effectively works in our lives, brings truth, builds us up, and gives us an eternal inheritance. What awesome power and amazing promises!

God's Word will transform your life only if you apply what you learn to your life.

James 1:21-25 — *Therefore, lay aside all filthiness and overflow of wickedness, and receive with meekness the implanted word, which is able to save your souls. But be doers of the word, and not hearers only, deceiving yourselves. For if anyone is a hearer of the word and not a doer, he is like a man observing his natural face in a mirror; for he observes himself, goes away, and immediately forgets what kind of man he was. But he who looks into the perfect law of liberty and continues in it, and is not a forgetful hearer but a doer of the work, this one will be blessed in what he does.*

We will be walking a journey together through the Word of God to learn how He transforms lives and brings hope and healing to His children who desire to know Him more intimately. God loves you, and He demonstrates His love all throughout the Bible, which is His written Word of hope for all people. Let's begin our journey together and see what He has in store for you.

Questions for Reflection:

What does Psalm 1:2–3 say will be the result if I meditate or spend time day and night thinking about God's Word?

_____

_____

_____

_____

_____

_____

_____

How often do I spend time reading and meditating on Scripture? What excuses do I use to avoid spending quality time reading, studying, and meditating on the Word of God?

_____

_____

_____

_____

_____

_____

_____

Application: What change am I willing to make in my daily life to spend more time meditating on God's Word?

_____

_____

_____

_____

_____

_____

_____

_____

Prayer: *Lord, forgive me for neglecting your Word and increase my desire to read and meditate on your Holy Scriptures. Help me overcome any fear I may have about what You might say to me and help me to understand Your Word and apply it to my life. Amen.*

My Thoughts/Reflections:

Day 2

God's Love

The Lord has appeared of old to me, saying:
"Yes, I have loved you with an everlasting love;
Therefore with lovingkindness I have drawn you."

Jeremiah 31:3

God loves you. Did you hear me? God loves you. It does not matter what you have done in your life, no matter how bad you think you are or how far you have strayed from God. He loves you. He loves you so much that He sent his only Son to die on a cross and take the punishment for your sins upon Himself, so you can be reconciled or reconnected to God. John 3:16 says, "God so loved the world that He gave His only begotten Son, that whoever believes in Him should not perish but have everlasting life." That is great news! God not only loves you, He knows every tiny detail about you because He created you just the way you are.

There is an enemy in this world whose intent is separating us from God. Sin entered the world in the Garden of Eden when Satan tempted Adam and Eve to rebel against God by doing the one thing God instructed Adam not to do. And they failed the test. (Read Genesis 2 and 3.) As a result, we were all born sinners (Romans 3:10; 3:23).

Satan has been trying to destroy you since you were born. The Bible says your enemy, the devil, prowls around like a roaring lion seeking someone to destroy (1 Peter 5:8). He is also referred to as the thief who comes to steal, kill and destroy (John 10:10). All the negative things people have said to you or about you over the years were messages from the one who did not want to see you reconciled to God. People who said you were not good enough, that you would never amount to anything, and that you don't belong were used as instruments by Satan to discourage you and separate you from God's truth about you.

The way to counteract these negative thoughts is to fill your mind and heart with the truth about you from God's Word! Read Psalm 139 and see what God says about you. He created you specifically and knows absolutely everything about you. He thinks about you and loves you. Isn't that amazing?

The Bible says that just like Jeremiah, you were known by God before He formed you in your mother's womb (Jeremiah 1:5). He has a plan and a purpose for your life. In order to walk in your destiny, you need to see yourself like God sees you, truly understand your worth, and refuse to listen to the voice of the enemy of your soul from this day forward.

Let God begin to show you His truth about your worth today. As you read, study and meditate on His Word, allow Him to speak to your heart and write down what He tells you. Journaling while reading God's Word is a great way to remember what He is saying to you and a great way to interact with God in prayer. When you come across Scriptures that encourage you and speak directly to your situation, try writing them down in a journal or notebook. Then write down how you feel about what you just read and write down any questions you have about the Scripture. Many times, God will answer your questions through journaling and prayer.

Questions for Reflection:

What lies have I believed about myself because of what other people have said or done to me that I now recognize as the enemy's attempt to prevent me from experiencing the love of God?

_____

_____

_____

_____

_____

_____

_____

What truths have I found in the Word of God to contradict these lies?

_____

_____

_____

_____

_____

_____

Application: Try writing out Psalm 139 as a personal prayer to God, inserting your comments in response to what the Scripture says to you and about you.

_____

_____

_____

_____

_____

_____

_____

_____

_____

Prayer: *Lord, please help me to experience Your love in a deeper way than I have ever known before. I have been seeking love from people and can never be fully satisfied by the love of this world. You say in Your Word that Your love for me is an everlasting love. Draw me closer to You as I spend time in Your Word and fully satisfy me with Your wonderful, unconditional love. Amen.*

My Thoughts/Reflections:

Day 3

FREEDOM IN TRUTH

*Then Jesus said to those Jews who believed Him,
"If you abide in My word, you are My disciples indeed.
And you shall know the truth, and the truth
shall make you free."*

John 8:31–32

Jesus forgives, rescues, sets free and heals when we bring our brokenness to him. The Bible says that when we confess our sins, He is faithful and just to forgive us of our sins and to cleanse us from all unrighteousness (1 John 1:9).

In numerous places in the Bible, people called out or reached out to Jesus in their brokenness and asked Him for help, and He never turned them away (Matthew 9:27–29; Mark 1:40–41; Luke 8:43–48; Matthew 20:29–34; Matthew 14:22–31). Also in many instances Jesus initiated the contact with a hurting person and healed them (John 5:1–9; Luke 13:10–13; John 4:1–26,28). Finally, there are instances where others assisted another person to get to Jesus for healing, or they came to Him for healing on behalf of someone else (Luke 5:17–26; John 4:46–54).

In addition to those who sought healing from Jesus, there were people (even religious leaders) who exposed others' sins for the sake of public humiliation, as well as trying to trap Jesus in His response, so they could justify killing Him (John 8:1–11). Other times, they did not physically expose the sinner, but harbored ill will toward them in their hearts, and Jesus consistently responded to the sinner with mercy, grace, and forgiveness (Luke 7:36–50). The Bible also reveals that some people are afflicted with infirmities, not because of sin in their lives, but because

God wants to use their lives and their testimony to reveal His glory. The story of the man who was blind from birth is one such example (John 9:1–11).

When others condemn you for what they see in your life, or you condemn yourself for your behavior, know that God is standing by to forgive you and cleanse you from all unrighteousness. He is waiting for you to expose your shortcomings to the light, to confess your sins to Him, and to allow Him to set you free, so He can begin to heal your pain.

God's Word is truth, and if you abide in His Word, He will show you the truth about who He is, and how much He loves you. The truth He wants you to understand and incorporate into every aspect of your being will transform your life forever!

Questions for Reflection:

What does John 8:31–32 say will happen if I abide or remain in God's Word?

_____

_____

_____

_____

_____

_____

_____

What truth(s) has God revealed to me in reviewing the Scriptures referenced in today's devotion that apply directly to my life?

_____

_____

_____

_____

_____

_____

_____

_____

Application: Bring to God one area of brokenness or a shortcoming in your life that He made you aware of in today's Scripture reading and ask for His forgiveness and healing touch.

Prayer: *Lord, thank you for showing me a shortcoming or area of my life that I need to confess and surrender to You for Your forgiveness and healing touch. Thank you for being a gracious and loving God who wants the best for me. Help me to abide in Your Word each day, so Your truth will truly make me free! Amen.*

My Thoughts/Reflections:

Day 4

HEARING GOD'S VOICE

*Now we have received, not the spirit of the world,
but the Spirit who is from God, that we
might know the things
that have been freely given to us by God.*

1 Corinthians 2:12

God first spoke to man shortly after He created the first human beings (Genesis 1:26–28). All throughout the Bible, we see instances where God spoke to people in various ways through:

- His Audible voice: Adam and Eve – Genesis 3; Samuel – 1 Samuel 3; Moses – Exodus 3; Abraham – Genesis 12; Elijah: 1 Kings 19:11–13; Gideon – Judges 6.
- His Prophets: Samuel to Saul – 1 Samuel 15; Nathan to David – 2 Samuel 12; Jonah to the people of Nineveh – Jonah 3.
- His Written Word: King Josiah – 2 Kings 22; People of Jerusalem – Nehemiah 8:1–11.

When Jesus walked this earth in human form, He communicated directly with humanity through His teachings and interactions with people. In the Book of John, Jesus reveals that He is the Good Shepherd and that His sheep know His voice (John 10:1–27). Jesus was saying, like sheep who know the voice of their shepherd (protector, provider, comforter), those who know Him as Lord and Savior know His voice.

As Jesus was nearing the end of His time on this earth, He promised that He would send the Holy Spirit to be with us and to speak to us after He departed this earth (John 14:25–26;

John 16:12–15; Hebrews 10:15–16; 1 Corinthians 2:9–12). The Holy Spirit speaks to us today through promptings in our spirit.

God has been speaking to mankind in various ways ever since He created us, and the Bible tells us that He is the same yesterday, today, and forever (Hebrews 13:8). Therefore, we can be sure that He is speaking to you and me today. We just need to be still and learn to listen and know His voice.

Some people find it helpful to have a special place to go and get away from the distractions of their daily lives where they feel closer to God to truly hear His voice, like out in nature, on a beach, in a quiet prayer closet or some other special place in their home or work place. Others like to listen to music to quiet their minds and hearts to hear from God, or they go for a run or walk. Sometimes it is the time of day that matters, like early morning or late at night when there are fewer distractions. The key is to figure out what works best for you and to make your communication with God a two-way conversation, both speaking to God and listening to Him.

When learning to hear the voice of God, keep in mind His character. God will never contradict His character when communicating with you. We know the character of God by studying His Word. You will know how God will react to circumstances and situations in your life by reading about how He has reacted to similar situations in the Bible.

Questions for Reflection:

In which ways has God spoken to me? Which of the Scriptures above can I best relate to in knowing that God was speaking to me?

_____

_____

_____

_____

_____

_____

_____

How much time do I spend each day truly listening to what God has to say to me?

_____

_____

_____

_____

_____

_____

_____

_____

Application: What change(s) will I make to improve the quality and/or quantity of time that I truly listen to what God has to say to me?

_____

_____

_____

_____

_____

_____

_____

_____

Prayer: *Lord, help me to be more sensitive to hear what You are saying to me. Please help me to make lasting changes in my life that keep me in a posture to listen to you more and to apply to my life what You tell me. Amen.*

My Thoughts/Reflections:

Day 5

COMMUNICATING WITH GOD

*Now this is the confidence that we have in Him,
that if we ask anything according to His will, He hears us.
And if we know that He hears us, whatever we ask,
we know that we have the petitions
that we have asked of Him.*

1 John 5:14–15

Prayer is one of the ways we communicate with God. We have already studied how God communicates with us. Now, we will focus on one of the ways we can communicate with God. As hard as it may be to comprehend, God really wants to hear from you. In fact, the Bible says we are to pray without ceasing (1 Thessalonians 5:17). By this, we are to always be in a posture of prayer—talking to God and listening to Him.

There are no special requirements for prayer. Some people are unsure, even fearful about prayer because they have never been taught how to pray. Or they have not spent time with others who are comfortable with prayer to learn from them. Some people think that God requires a special formula or eloquent words to be spoken before He will listen and respond. Nothing could be further from the truth! If you don't believe me, let's look at some prayers in the Bible that were not lengthy or eloquent and were still answered by God:

"Lord, save me!" (Matthew 14:30)

"Now Hannah spoke in her heart; only her lips moved, but her voice was not heard…" (1 Samuel 1:13)

"Jesus, Son of David, have mercy on me!" (Luke 18:38)

"Therefore, give to Your servant an understanding heart to judge Your people, that I may discern between good and evil. For who is able to judge this great people of Yours?" (1 Kings 3:9)

God wants to hear from you. Prayer is a means to develop an intimate relationship with Him. Just like you spend time talking to your friends about everything in your life, talking to God about those same things is prayer. The Bible tells us that if we develop intimacy with Him and know His Word, our will becomes aligned with the will of God, and we can ask for whatever we want and it will be given to us (John 15:7).

Even when we don't know what to pray for or how to pray, God has already given every born-again Christian His Holy Spirit who makes intercession for us in accordance with the will of God (Romans 8:26–27). That is great news! God even gives us what we need to communicate with Him in prayer. If you do not already have a regular prayer life, begin right now and your life will never be the same!

Questions for Reflection:

What have I believed about prayer that has kept me from developing intimacy with God through prayer?

_____

_____

_____

_____

_____

_____

_____

What would change about my prayer life if I truly believed that God hears my every prayer?

_____

_____

_____

_____

_____

_____

_____

_____

Application: Today, when you would normally reach out to a friend, teacher, counselor, pastor or family member about something you are wrestling with or a decision you need to make, talk to God about it first in prayer.

Prayer: *Lord, I confess that I often think of You last when I am seeking counsel or advice. Please help me to make a new habit of going to You first in prayer with every issue I am struggling with and every decision I need to make, both big and small. Amen.*

My Thoughts/Reflections:

Day 6

UNDERSTANDING THE ROOT CAUSES OF SIN

*Therefore do not let sin reign in your mortal body,
that you should obey it in its lusts.*

Romans 6:12

You may know the story of Adam and Eve, the first two humans God created and placed in the Garden of Eden where the serpent (devil) tempted them to eat of the tree of knowledge of good and evil, which God specifically prohibited them from eating (Genesis 2:1–17; 3:1–6). At that moment, sin entered into the world and has been passed down through all generations of humanity (Romans 3:10; 3:23). As a result of their sin—and to keep them from eating of the tree of life and remaining in sin forever—God banished Adam and Eve from the Garden to protect them (Genesis 3:22–24).

You and I were born into sin—so were our parents, our grandparents, our brothers and sisters, our teachers, our coaches, our pastors, our _____ you name it; we were all born into sin. As you well know from your own life, sinners have a natural propensity to remain in the flesh and sin. Therefore, people get hurt as a result of these sinful interactions with one another. Sometimes, people hurt other people on purpose. At other times, it is not done with any kind of intent; it just happens.

Hurts can propel people into life-controlling sinful behaviors if they do not surrender their lives to the Lordship of Jesus Christ. These can be any number of things like addictions, sexual immorality, self-harm, anger, to name a few. After the Fall of Adam, the story continues, and the remainder of the Bible is about God's marvelous plan for reconciling us to Him through the sacrificial love of Jesus who died on the cross for our sins, so we could be restored to God through justification and the free gift of righteousness (Romans 5:16–19). In the end, when all is said and done, all people who accepted Jesus Christ as Lord and Savior and allowed God to transform their lives, so they could live holy and pleased God will be saved and will have access to the tree of life as God makes all things new (Romans 10:9; 10:23; Revelation 21:1–8; 22:1–5).

When we truly surrender our lives to Jesus and allow the Holy Spirit to guide and direct every part of our lives, we have the power to overcome sin. If we walk in the Spirit, we will not fulfill the sinful desires of the flesh (Galatians 5:16).

Questions for Reflection:

Who or what have I been blaming for my sinful behaviors?

_____

_____

_____

_____

_____

_____

_____

What area(s) of my life have I not fully surrendered to the Lordship of Jesus Christ?

_____

_____

_____

_____

_____

_____

_____

_____

_____

Application: Today I will pray a prayer of repentance. I will seek God's forgiveness for not allowing the Holy Spirit complete access to every area of my life, especially the area(s) that He revealed to me just now. I will commit to allowing the Holy Spirit free reign in my life every day from this day forward.

Prayer: *Lord, thank you for bringing to my mind the area(s) of sin in my life that I need to repent of and ask for Your forgiveness. Help me to walk in the Spirit today and every day, so I do not fulfill the sinful desires of my flesh. Amen.*

My Thoughts/Reflections:

Day 7

SALVATION

*For God so loved the world that
He gave His only begotten Son,
that whoever believes in Him should not perish
but have everlasting life. For God did not send His Son
into the world to condemn the world,
but that the world through Him might be saved.*

John 3:16–17

What is salvation? Why do I need it? What do I need to do to be saved? Salvation is a broad term referring to God's activity in bringing all things to God's intended goal. More specifically, salvation entails God's deliverance of humans from the power and effects of sin and the Fall through the work of Jesus Christ, so creation in general and humans in particular can enjoy the fullness of life intended for what God has made (Grenz *Pocket Dictionary of Theological Terms*).

As sinners separated from God due to the Fall of man (Genesis 3:1–24) and our own sin, we had no way on our own to get back into a right relationship with God (Romans 3:10; 3:23). However, from the very beginning, God had a plan to restore that broken relationship! Someone had to pay the penalty due for our sin, and the payment required was death (Romans 6:23).

God's amazing plan involved His only begotten Son Jesus Christ. He left His throne in heaven to live on earth as a human being, fully God and fully man, but to do so without sin (Hebrews 4:15). Jesus died in our place to atone for and pay the price for our sin. His blood washes us clean and makes us acceptable to God the Father (Hebrews 10:19). Not only did Jesus die on the cross for my sins and yours, but also God raised Him from the dead and He ascended into heaven where He now sits at the right hand of the Father, making intercession for us (Romans 8:34).

How does a person acquire this salvation? The Bible says there is nothing we can do to obtain this salvation apart from believing by faith in God's grace alone to extend to us this free gift of salvation (Romans 6:23; Ephesians 2:8). Salvation is available to all who express penitent and obedient faith in Jesus Christ as Lord (Romans 10:9–10,13).

Salvation covers all of our sins. Believers are freed from the penalty of sins of the past (Ephesians 2:5). We are free from the power of sin in the present (Philippians 1:6). And we will be free from the presence of sin in the future as all those who are saved will be glorified and live eternally without sin (1 Peter 1:5). Jesus Christ alone is the author and finisher of our faith, and there is no other name under the heavens whereby we can be saved, except the name of Jesus Christ (Acts 4:12; John 14:6).

Questions for Reflection:

When did I first become aware that I was separated from God because of my sin, and what did I do about it?

_____

_____

_____

_____

_____

_____

_____

Who do I know who would benefit from knowing what I know about this free gift of salvation?

_____

_____

_____

_____

_____

_____

_____

_____

_____

Application: Pray and ask God to reveal to you some unique ways to share your faith in Jesus Christ with people close to you who do not know Him

Prayer: *Lord, thank you for sending Jesus to atone for my sins and for showing me the way to salvation! Help me to be bold in sharing my faith with others, so they too can be saved in the precious name of Jesus. Amen.*

My Thoughts/Reflections:

Day 8

Forgiving Others

*Let all bitterness, wrath, anger, clamor, and evil speaking
be put away from you, with all malice.
And be kind to one another, tenderhearted,
forgiving one another, even as God in Christ forgave you.*

Ephesians 4:31–32

Forgiveness is a gift we want from God when we sin against Him, but not one that we can easily give to people who hurt us. Most people find it very difficult to forgive someone who has hurt them, and they hold on to that hurt—recalling it over and over in their minds, sometimes for years. That hurt and pain becomes like a type of cancer. After reliving the incident for a period of time, they bury it deep inside where it festers below the surface, causing damage to their physical health and well-being, not to mention their relationships with others. Studies suggest that holding on to un-forgiveness affects the immune system and can lead to chronic pain, heart disease, cancer, and other ailments.

God places a high value on forgiveness—an incredibly high value—demonstrated by the fact that He sent His Son Jesus to die on the cross for the forgiveness of your sins and mine. The Bible says, "For if you forgive men their trespasses, your heavenly Father will also forgive you. But if you do not forgive men their trespasses, neither will your Father forgive your trespasses" (Matthew 6:14–15).

God also gives us a timeframe in which to forgive when someone has hurt us. The Bible says, "Be angry, and do not sin: do not let the sun go down on your wrath, nor give place to the devil" (Ephesians 4:26–27). We are to forgive the trespasses of our offenders before the end of the day. Paul spoke to the Corinthians regarding forgiveness as follows: "Now whom you forgive anything, I also forgive. For if indeed I have forgiven anything, I have forgiven that one for your sakes in the presence of Christ, lest Satan should take advantage of us; for we are not ignorant of his devices" (2 Corinthians 2:10–11). Don't you know that Satan loves unforgiveness? What better way to keep Christians in bondage to pain and suffering? What better way to keep us from forgiving those who have hurt us and prevent restoration of our relationships with one another?

Bishop T.D. Jakes says, "Forgiveness is a gift you give to yourself," and he is right about that! Oftentimes, we hold on to unforgiveness for so long that the person who has hurt us has moved on with his life, oblivious to the pain we are still holding on to as a result of something he did, said, or failed to do or say. The unforgiveness hurts only the one who is holding on to it.

Questions for Reflection:

What are the name(s) of all the people I can think of who have offended me, and that I have not forgiven?

_____

_____

_____

_____

_____

_____

Do I have any unforgiveness toward God for the things I have experienced in my life?

_____

_____

_____

_____

_____

_____

_____

Application: Think of one person whom you have not forgiven for what they did or failed to do. Write a letter to God expressing your *attitude of forgiveness*, your willingness to forgive that person regardless of whether they have asked for forgiveness or not, even if they have passed away and are no longer alive. Completely release that person from the offense(s) in your letter to God. Be specific. At the end of your letter, write a prayer of blessing over the life of the person who has offended you. Pray that God will bless them (Matthew 5:44) and ask God to heal your heart from the pain of the offense.

_____

_____

_____

_____

_____

_____

_____

_____

_____

_____

Prayer: *Lord, please forgive me for harboring unforgiveness in my heart toward _____. I release them and ask you to bless them. My desire is to be close to You and live a life pleasing to You. Amen.*

My Thoughts/Reflections:

Day 9

FORGIVING OURSELVES

I, even I, am He who blots out your transgressions
for My own sake;
And I will not remember your sins.
Put Me in remembrance;
Let us contend together;
State your case, that you may be acquitted.

Isaiah 43:25–26

Do you harbor feelings of guilt and self-condemnation for things you have done or failed to do, for things you still struggle with that you know are not pleasing to God, and for feeling as though your sins are unforgiveable? I have great news for you! Forgiveness is a not a feeling; it is a biblical truth. God's forgiveness is a gift to man as part of our salvation for the blotting out of our transgressions, so we can be restored to Him through the shed atoning blood of Jesus Christ. God's forgiveness has erased our sins—past, present, and future—as if they never occurred (Isaiah 43:25–26; Hebrews 10:17; Psalm 103:12; 130:3–4).

This does not mean that after salvation we will never sin again. God knows our human frailties and, therefore, He has made provisions for us. When we do sin, we are to go to God, confess our sins, repent, and ask for forgiveness. He is faithful and just to forgive us and completely cleanse us from all unrighteousness (1 John 1:9). God does not replay the sins He has forgiven and bring them up against us again and again. So why are we so hard on ourselves? Why do we feel guilty and condemn ourselves when we sin? Why do we play the movie again and again in our minds? Maybe because it is so hard for us to forgive others, and we believe that our imperfect forgiveness of others is equivalent to God's forgiveness of our sins. Or, perhaps, because we don't fully understand and fully embrace the forgiveness that God has bestowed upon us.

In order to be free from the guilt and self-condemnation related to our sin is to understand and embrace the amazing grace of God. "Grace perfects forever the saved one in the sight of God because of the saved one's position 'in Christ.' Grace bestows Christ's merit and Christ's standing forever" *(The New Unger's Bible Dictionary)*. By grace, we are saved through faith in Jesus Christ (Ephesians 2:8). We can't work for forgiveness or salvation; these are bestowed upon us by the grace of God. We just need to have faith and believe the Word of God, which says that God will forgive our sins when we repent and ask for His forgiveness. He will blot out the memory of our sin as if it never occurred.

To reiterate, forgiveness is not a feeling. If you don't *feel* forgiven for the sins you have committed, despite asking God for His forgiveness, you must accept God's forgiveness by faith. Think about the incredibly high price that God paid for the forgiveness of your sins. He sacrificed His one and only son, Jesus Christ, who shed His blood for the remission of your sins (Matthew 26:28; Ephesians 1:7). God will not withhold his forgiveness from you if you truly repent and ask for His forgiveness (1 John 1:9).

Questions for Reflection:

What does God say I should do in Isaiah 43:25–26?

_____

_____

_____

_____

_____

_____

_____

What sin(s) do I need to bring to God for forgiveness?

_____

_____

_____

_____

_____

_____

_____

Application: Today I will examine my life for any past or present sins I have not forgiven myself for and bring these to the Lord in prayer for His forgiveness and cleansing.

Prayer: *Lord, please search my heart for any areas of unforgiveness, especially areas that I have refused to release myself from, and that are holding me back from being all that You have planned for my life. Give me the courage to release these to You and to believe by faith that I am completely forgiven. Amen.*

My Thoughts/Reflections:

Day 10

Key to Life is Death to Self

*Therefore, if anyone is in Christ,
he is a new creation;
old things have passed away;
behold, all things have become new.*

2 Corinthians 5:17

Marketing firms offer many remedies to achieve a new life of satisfaction and purpose through travel, career changes, educational pursuits, the acquisition of material possessions, and other means.

The Bible tells us that Jesus died on the cross, so we could have new life—a life no longer controlled by the ways of this world, but by the Spirit that makes us new creations in Him! If we remain *in Christ*, we die to our former way of life—*old things have passed away*—and *all things become new*, making us new creations with a new outlook on life and a new power to live a life that is pleasing to God. We are able to experience the abundant life that Jesus died to give us now and for all eternity!

To be *in Christ* means we surrender our whole life to His Lordship. Every day we need to die to self and yield our mind, our will, our emotions, our bodies, our finances, our plans, our desires, our future, our everything to Jesus. When we abide in Him, the old things in our lives must die. We no longer operate from our own understanding. We instead seek the direction and guidance for our lives from God.

John 12:24 says unless a grain of wheat falls into the ground and dies, it remains alone; but if it dies, it produces much grain. The impact and effectiveness of a single grain of wheat is greatly multiplied only if it dies to what it formerly was. This is also what happens to us when we die to our former selves and allow God to transform our lives and fulfill the plans and purposes He intended for us. Our new life *in Christ* looks as different as the grain of wheat that goes into the ground from the plant that arises from the soil when that seed dies to self.

The amazing thing is that we do not have to work or perform or strive for this new life. All we have to do is surrender and remain *in Christ*. John 15:4 says we are to abide in Christ and allow Him to abide in us. Just as the branch cannot bear fruit of itself unless it abides in the vine, neither can we unless we abide in Him. Jesus is the Vine, and He freely gives us everything we need for new life.

Questions for Reflection:

Have I truly been living my life *in Christ*, or have I retained control of some area(s) of my life?

_____
_____
_____
_____
_____
_____
_____
_____

What new thing(s) does God want to do in my life that I have been resisting?

_____
_____
_____
_____
_____
_____
_____
_____

Application: Imagine what would happen if you surrendered an area of your life, that you have retained control of, to the Lordship of Jesus Christ. Envision how He will bring new life out of your obedience.

_____

_____

_____

_____

_____

_____

_____

_____

Prayer: *Lord, today I surrender every aspect of my life to you. I ask you to guide and direct my thoughts and actions throughout this day. I choose today to die to my old selfish desires, to the ways of this world, and to allow you to lead me into the new and abundant life that Jesus died on the cross to secure for me. Amen.*

My Thoughts/Reflections:

Day 11

WALKING IN INTEGRITY

*No temptation has overtaken you
except such as is common to man;
but God is faithful, who will not allow you to be tempted
beyond what you are able, but with the temptation
will also make the way of escape,
that you may be able to bear it.*

1 Corinthians 10:13

What is integrity? The definition of *integrity* is steadfast adherence to a strict moral or ethical code; the quality or condition of being whole or undivided *(The American Heritage Dictionary of the English Language)*. Therefore, integrity requires that we maintain a steadfast adherence to biblical laws and principles with respect to our conduct. The Word of God should be the authority with which we govern our lives.

In every area of life, we can represent Christ well by living a life of integrity, or we can succumb to the temptations of the world and slip into the sins of indulging the flesh such as sexual immorality, gluttony, drug and alcohol abuse, anger, fits of rage, just to name a few. At all times, I must maintain a Christ-centered standard of conduct while in the presence of other Christians and while around people who do not know me, even when nobody else is around.

Amazingly, God knows all about temptation! The Bible says Jesus was tempted, just as we are, but was without sin (Hebrews 4:15). Sexual immorality—one area of sin—is particularly prevalent in our society today. We know from the Word of God that absolutely no sexual conduct is authorized by God outside the confines of marriage between one man and one woman. We live in a highly sexually charged world. You cannot watch television, listen to the radio, pick up a magazine, or go on the internet without being constantly bombarded with sexually charged stimuli. That is because we live in a fallen world that rages from the effects of sin. People of the world follow after the lusts of the flesh and perpetuate this addiction through all forms of media. But we are called to be set apart from the world. God's will for us is our sanctification: that we should abstain from sexual immorality and know how to possess our bodies in sanctification and honor, not in passion of lust, like those who do not know God (1 Thessalonians 4:3–5). We also have a promise from God: no temptation has overtaken you except such as is common to man; but God is faithful, who will not allow you to be tempted beyond what you are able, but with the temptation He will also make the way of escape, that you may be able to bear it (1 Corinthians 10:13).

We need to be sensitive to the Spirit to see the ways of escape that God sets before us when we are tempted to sin Therefore, do not let sin reign in your mortal body, that you should obey it in its lusts. And do not present your members as instruments of unrighteousness to sin, but present yourselves to God as being alive from the dead, and your members as instruments of righteousness to God. For sin shall not have dominion over you, for you are not under law but under grace (Romans 6:11–14).

If we are serious about living a life of integrity, even after we have removed the things that feed our carnal nature, have disassociated ourselves from the people we used to sin with, have stopped going to the places we used to go to that enabled us to sin, and we have done everything we know to do to put guards in place to protect us, we will still face temptations that will challenge us to revert back to our old habits. While you will not be protected from temptations that come your way, you must know that God will ALWAYS make a way of escape for you when you are faced with such temptations. "No temptation has overtaken you except such as is common to man; but God is faithful, who will not allow you to be tempted beyond what you are able, but with the temptation will also make the way of escape, that you may be able to bear it" (1 Corinthians 10:13). Isn't it incredible to know that God knows what you can bear? You may think you are being tempted beyond what you can overcome, but God created you and knows you better than you know yourself. Look for the escape route He provides to you EVERY time you are tempted.

Furthermore, James 1:12 says, "Blessed is the man who endures temptation; for when he has been approved, he will receive the crown of life, which the Lord has promised to those who love Him." God encourages us to *endure* temptations when they arise. *Endure* means to bear with tolerance, or suffer patiently without yielding *(The American Heritage Dictionary of the English Language)*. You CAN endure the temptations that come your way. And when you do, you will be rewarded. These temptations are temporary attempts by the enemy to get you to satisfy your flesh. When Satan is unsuccessful in his attempts to get you to revert back and dishonor God, he will leave. The Word of God says, "Resist the devil and he will flee from you" (James 4:7). Resist the enemy of your soul and use the escape route that God has provided to you! Each time you endure the temptation and do not sin, you become stronger and stronger in the Lord.

Questions for Reflection:

In which area(s) of my life have I not been walking in integrity?

___

What warning signs has God given me and what *ways of escape* has He made available to me that I have ignored the last time I was tempted to follow the lusts of my flesh and sin?

___

Application: Write down two or three practical things you can begin to do differently today to be more sensitive to the Spirit of God, so you can follow the escape path when you are tempted to sin.

_____

_____

_____

_____

_____

_____

Prayer: *Lord, forgive me for ignoring your warning signs and failing to follow the escape path you prepared for me when I was last tempted to fulfill the lusts of my flesh. Help me, Lord, for my desire is to walk in integrity and govern every area of my life by your Word. Amen.*

My Thoughts/Reflections:

Day 12

SPIRITUAL WARFARE

*For though we walk in the flesh,
we do not war according to the flesh.
For the weapons of our warfare are not carnal
but mighty in God for pulling down strongholds,
casting down arguments and every high thing
that exalts itself against the knowledge of God,
bringing every thought into captivity*

to the obedience of Christ,

2 Corinthians 10:3–5

Spiritual warfare is an obstacle every Christian faces. In fact, the Word of God says we should not be surprised when fiery trials come into our lives, as though something strange were happening to us (1 Peter 4:12). When you accept Jesus Christ as Lord of your life, walk away from the things of the world, and turn your attention and your life toward the things of God, you become a target for the enemy who wants you back under his dominion and control.

The Bible tells us to be self-controlled and alert because the devil prowls around like a roaring lion seeking someone to devour (1 Peter 5:8). We must understand how the enemy operates, so he cannot take advantage of us (2 Corinthians 2:11). Thankfully, the Bible gives us instructions on how to identify the works of the enemy and how to arm ourselves for spiritual battle. The devil is a liar and the father of lies (John 8:44). He will tempt us to sin, and then try to convince us that God will not forgive us when we do. We need to understand the battle plans of the enemy of our souls, and we need to know the Truth of God's

Word. He (Jesus) who is in us is greater than he (Satan) who is in the world (1 John 4:4).

Spiritual battles must be fought with spiritual tools. The full armor of God, as identified in Ephesians 6:10–18, provides spiritual protection when we face spiritual warfare: "Put on the whole armor of God, that you may be able to stand against the wiles of the devil. For we do not wrestle against flesh and blood, but against principalities, against powers, against the rulers of the darkness of this age, against spiritual *hosts* of wickedness in the heavenly *places*" (Ephesians 6:11–12).

I must gird my waist with the belt of truth (v. 14). This refers to the Truth of God's Word, and it is the central piece of armor to which the breastplate of righteousness is attached (v. 14). The breastplate guards my heart and makes me secure in the knowledge that I am in right standing with God because of what Jesus did for me in dying on the cross to cover my sins. I must shod my feet with the preparation of the gospel of peace (v. 15), which helps me to stand firm in the face of the attacks of the enemy, knowing that I do not have to run and that I have peace in my relationship with Jesus. Then I must take up the shield of faith with which I will be able to quench all the fiery darts of the wicked one (v. 16). The devil will shoot fiery darts at me, but the shield of faith will protect me. My faith and trust in God extinguishes (snuffs out) all that the devil throws my way. The helmet of salvation (v. 17) protects my mind from the lies that the enemy tries to plant there to make me doubt God. When my mind is protected, I am at peace. I am to take up the sword of the Spirit, which is the Word of God (v. 17). This is the only offensive piece of my armor, meaning I can use it to attack the enemy. Memorizing Scripture and knowing what God's Word says will help me to ward off the attacks of the enemy of my soul. Finally, I am to pray—always praying all prayer and supplication in the Spirit (v. 18).

Spiritual warfare is real, and every Christian will have to face it. But God has not left us without knowledge of the tactics of the enemy, nor the weapons to use to successfully fight. It is our responsibility to use what God has given us to fight these battles until He returns or takes us home.

Questions for Reflection:

When was the last time I was caught off guard by the enemy who tried to destroy me?

_____

_____

_____

_____

_____

_____

What can I learn or be reminded of about the tactics of the enemy of my soul regarding that experience?

_____

_____

_____

_____

_____

_____

_____

_____

Application: Meditatively read Ephesians 6:10–18 and pray about each piece of spiritual armor, asking God to help you to daily apply each one to your life.

Prayer: *Lord, help me to put on Your spiritual armor today and every day. Remind me that Your weapons are powerful for pulling down strongholds in my life and in the lives of my family members. Your weapons are also for casting down arguments and every high thing that exalts itself against the knowledge of God. Help me to bring every thought that I have into captivity to the obedience of Christ. Amen.*

My Thoughts/Reflections:

Day 13

THE HEART

Keep your heart with all diligence,
For out of it spring the issues of life.

Proverbs 4:23

When Scripture refers to the *heart*, it is not referring to the physical muscle in your chest that pumps blood throughout your body. According to the *New Unger's Bible Dictionary*, the word *heart* in Scripture means a variety of things, including:

- The center of the bodily life, the reservoir of the entire life-power (Psalm 40:8,10,12)
- The center of the rational-spiritual nature of man (Esther 7:5; 1 Corinthians 7:37)
- The seat of love and hatred (1 Timothy 1:5; Leviticus 19:17)
- The center of moral life, from the highest love of God to the hardening of the heart (Psalm 73:26; Isaiah 6:10; Jeremiah 16:12)
- The laboratory and origin of all that is good and evil in thoughts, words, and deeds (Matthew 12:34; Mark 7:21)
- The rendezvous of evil lusts and passions (Romans 1:24)
- The seat of conscience (Hebrews 10:22; 1 John 3:19–21)

Many of the references above are tied to emotions. Other references to the heart in Scripture reveal that it is also tied to the mind or intellect of a person, and it can understand (John

12:40; Ephesians 1:8). The heart is also tied to the will of a person (Exodus 25:2; 35:5).

Additionally, the heart is closely connected with the *soul* having, as one meaning, the seat of the feelings, desires, affections, and aversions of a person *(New Unger's Bible Dictionary)*. In other words, the heart is tied to the conscience of a person.

As you can see, the scriptural heart is very closely tied to the mind, will, emotions, and conscience of a person. God has said repeatedly in His Word that we are to love Him and serve Him with our whole heart (Deuteronomy 6:5; 11:13; 13:3; Joshua 22:5; Jeremiah 29:13; Matthew 22:37; Mark 12:30; Luke 10:27). In order to love and serve Him well, we must have our hearts right with God.

Proverbs 27:19 says, "As in water face reflects face, so a man's heart reveals the man." Therefore, it is extremely important that our hearts are pure and clean. "Create in me a clean heart, O God, and renew a steadfast spirit within me" (Psalm 51:10). We also must be very careful not to allow our hearts to become hard and incapable of receiving the love and affection of God (Ephesians 4:18; Proverbs 28:14).

If you have allowed your heart to become hard and calloused as a result of the things you have experienced in your life, there is great news! God is in the business of heart transplants: "I will give you a new heart and put a new spirit within you; I will take the heart of stone out of your flesh and give you a heart of flesh" (Ezekiel 36:26).

Questions for Reflection:

What is the condition of my heart?

_____
_____
_____
_____
_____
_____
_____
_____
_____

Do I love God with my whole heart—mind, will, and emotions?

_____
_____
_____
_____
_____
_____
_____
_____
_____
_____

Application: Based on the Scriptures I reviewed today regarding my spiritual heart, I recognize that my heart needs work in the following area(s): _____. I lift these shortcomings to God and ask Him to make me more sensitive to His guidance in these areas.

Prayer: *Lord, my desire is to have a soft and receptive heart to the leading and guiding of Your Spirit. Help me to keep my heart with all diligence, so out of it spring only those things that are pleasing to You. Amen.*

My Thoughts/Reflections:

Day 14

My Hiding Place

You are my hiding place;
You shall preserve me from trouble;
You shall surround me with songs of deliverance. Selah
I will instruct you and teach you in the way you should go;
I will guide you with My eye.

Psalm 32:7–8

Sometimes life can become overwhelming. The day-to-day troubles of this world can overtake us and make us feel like we need to find a safe place to hide away to rest and recuperate. King David certainly felt this way, and he along with other Scripture writers referred to God as providing a hiding place in the midst of trouble (Psalm 17:8; 27:5; 31:20; 119:114; Proverbs 18:10; Isaiah 25:4).

Not only does God provide a hiding place, when we run to Him, He preserves us from trouble. We are safe in the shadow of His wings (Psalm 36:7; 57:1; 63:7; 91:4). Imagine being a baby bird, shielded from danger under the shadow of the wings of a parent bird. Where we are weak, He is strong.

To be surrounded by songs of deliverance implies great joy in the Lord's protection and preservation. When God delivered His children from trouble, they often sang and danced to celebrate the great victories of God. We see this in the Book of Exodus where God opened a path of dry ground in the middle of the sea to deliver His children out of slavery in Egypt. Moses sang a song of deliverance in Exodus Chapter 15, followed by his sister Miriam, who led a joyous dance with singing and tambourines to commemorate the great deliverance of the Lord (Exodus 15:20–21).

After we run to God for protection and preservation, and joyously celebrate Him for keeping us safe and delivering us from evil, He can instruct us and teach us the way that we should go (Psalm 32:8). He now has our full attention! The Scripture says that God will guide us with His eye. That means He always has His eyes on us. Just like a mother looks at her child from afar to guide him in the way he should go just by a glance of her eye, God will direct us if we will keep our focus on Him.

Questions for Reflection:

Who or what do I instinctively run to when I am overwhelmed or in trouble?

_____

_____

_____

_____

_____

_____

_____

Think about the last time you sought refuge in something or someone other than God. What do you think would have been the outcome of that situation if you went to God first?

_____

_____

_____

_____

_____

_____

_____

Application: Today make a concentrated effort to allow God to direct you with His eye. Keep your focus on Him and allow Him to direct all your decision-making this day.

Prayer: *Lord, thank you for being my hiding place, and my refuge in times of trouble. Help me to keep my focus on You, Lord, so I can take direction from You for every area of my life. Amen.*

My Thoughts/Reflections:

Day 15

OUR AUTHORITY IN CHRIST

*"Most assuredly, I say to you,
he who believes in Me, the works that I do he will do also;
and greater works than these he will do,
because I go to My Father. And whatever you ask in My name,
that I will do, that the Father may be glorified in the Son.
If you ask anything in My name, I will do it.*

John 14:12–14

If you have surrendered your life to Jesus and truly accepted Him as Lord and Savior, you already have the power and authority of Jesus' name to cast out demons and walk in complete victory over the attacks of the enemy. You are no longer a slave to sin. You have God's Power within you to face any challenge the enemy may throw your way. The Bible says, "You are of God little children, and have overcome them (ungodly spirits), because He (Spirit of God) who is in you is greater than he who is in the world" (1 John 4:4).

We read in the Scriptures where Jesus sent His disciples out in pairs and instructed them to heal the sick, cleanse lepers, raise the dead, and cast out demons (Matthew 10:1–4; Mark 6:7; Luke 9:1–3). Jesus taught His disciples saying, "Most assuredly, I say to you, he who believes in Me, the works that I do he will do also; and greater works than these he will do, because I go to My Father. And whatever you ask in My name, that I will do, that the Father may be glorified in the Son. If you ask anything in My name, I will do it" (John 14:12–14). He also teaches us to resist the enemy and draw near to God (James 4:7–8). God is the one who will fight for us.

We are not to fear the enemy. Jesus has already defeated Satan when He was crucified, died, was buried, rose from the dead, and is now seated at the right hand of the Father in heaven. Jesus will finally cast Satan into the lake of fire for all eternity at the appointed time (Revelation 20:2–3,7,10). Furthermore, God's Word assures us that nothing can harm us or separate us from His love. Who shall separate us from the love of Christ? Shall tribulation, or distress, or persecution, or famine, or nakedness, or peril, or sword? As it is written, "For Your sake we are killed all day long; We are accounted as sheep for the slaughter." Yet in all these things, we are more than conquerors through Him who loved us. For I am persuaded that neither death nor life, nor angels nor principalities nor powers, nor things present nor things to come, nor height nor depth, nor any other created thing, shall be able to separate us from the love of God which is in Christ Jesus our Lord (Romans 8:35–39).

Questions for Reflection:

Do I live each day as though the power of God is already within me to face any challenge that comes my way? Why or Why not?

_____

_____

_____

_____

_____

_____

_____

What do you think hinders Christians today from experiencing the amazing miracles we read about in the Bible?

_____

_____

_____

_____

_____

_____

_____

_____

Application: Think of a situation in your life when you did not exercise the spiritual authority you had in Christ and allowed the enemy to temporarily defeat you. How would you handle that situation today knowing that you already have all you need to defeat the enemy?

_____

_____

_____

_____

_____

_____

_____

_____

Prayer: *Lord, thank you for extending to me your authority and power to face the attacks of the enemy. Help me to remember my authority in Christ and to know that You have already defeated him and that nothing can ever separate me from your love! Amen.*

My Thoughts/Reflections:

Day 16

Removing Hindrances to Effective Prayer

*If My people who are called by My name
will humble themselves, and pray and seek My face,
and turn from their wicked ways, then I will hear from heaven,
and will forgive their sin and heal their land.
Now My eyes will be open and My ears attentive
to prayer made in this place.*

2 Chronicles 7:14–15

Prayer is the expression of man's dependence upon God for all things *(The New Unger's Bible Dictionary)*. It is essentially our lifeline to God. It is, therefore, vitally important that our prayers are getting through to God, that He hears us and answers our prayers.

The Bible reveals a number of hindrances or barriers to effective prayer. If we can identify any of these barriers in our lives, with God's help we can remove them, so we can effectively communicate with Him through prayer and receive the blessings and provision that He has for us.

God requires us to be obedient to His Word (1 Samuel 15:22). We can cry out to God day and night in prayer, but if we harbor certain sins in our lives, they will block our communication channel with God, and He will not answer our prayers. Some of the sins that create barriers or hindrances to prayer are:

- Unforgiveness (Matthew 18:23–35; Mark 11:25)
- Unbelief (James 1:5–7; Hebrews 11:6)
- Unrepentant sin (Isaiah 59:1–2; Psalm 66:18)
- Continued willful sin (Hebrews 10:26–27)
- Pride (Job 35:12,13)
- Hypocrisy (Job 27:8,9)
- Selfishness (James 4:3)

There are numerous examples in the Bible of the people of God who have sinned and as a result, God did not answer their prayers or the prayers of those praying on their behalf. (See Joshua 7:1–12; 2 Samuel 12:13–23; 1 Samuel 14:37; Numbers 20:7–12; 27:14). Elsewhere in the Word of God, we are told explicitly the things that will hinder our prayer life with God.

A healthy vibrant intimate relationship with God requires a clear communication channel between us and God. Let's examine our lives to see where we need to make changes to improve our ability to communicate with and experience intimacy with God, so we can receive the blessings and provision that come to us as a result of prayer.

Questions for Reflection:

How healthy is my current prayer life? Am I effectively communicating with and hearing from God?

_____

_____

_____

_____

_____

_____

_____

Based on the Scriptures above, what sin(s) are creating a barrier for me to effectively pray?

_____

_____

_____

_____

_____

_____

_____

_____

_____

Application: Repent of any areas of sin in your life that are hindering your prayer life and document practical steps that you will take to ensure that the sin(s) that are hindering your prayers will not enter into or creep back into your life and block effective communication and intimacy with God.

Prayer: *Lord, help me to keep my life in order, so I can effectively communicate with you. Convict me of any areas of sin that create a hindrance for me to develop and maintain intimacy with you, and I will repent and ask for your forgiveness, for intimacy with You is my greatest desire! Amen.*

My Thoughts/Reflections:

Day 17

HOLY SPIRIT'S POWER FOR INNER HEALING

*Likewise the Spirit also helps in our weaknesses.
For we do not know what we should pray for as we ought,
but the Spirit Himself makes intercession for us
with groanings which cannot be uttered.
Now He who searches the hearts knows
what the mind of the Spirit is,
because He makes intercession
for the saints according to the will of God.*

Romans 8:26–27

Who or what is the Holy Spirit? I believe that this member of the Godhead is the least known and understood. We seem to have a much better understanding about God the Father and God the Son (Jesus) than we do about God the Holy Spirit. It is important to learn about this powerful helper/counselor who has been freely given to every believer who has accepted Jesus Christ as Lord and Savior to guide our daily lives and transform us from the inside out.

There are several instances in the Bible when all three persons of the Trinity are mentioned together (Matthew 3:16–17; Matthew 28:19; 2 Corinthians 13:14; Titus 3:4–6). The most notable instance is when Jesus was baptized in the Jordan River by John the Baptist. "When He had been baptized, Jesus [God the Son] came up immediately from the water; and behold, the heavens were opened to Him, and He saw the Spirit of God [God the Holy Spirit] descending like a dove and alighting upon Him. And suddenly a voice came from heaven [God the Father], saying, "This is My beloved Son, in whom I am well pleased" (Matthew 3:16–17).

The Holy Spirit (or Holy Ghost) is a person, not an amorphous "*it*." He is God. In Acts 5:3–4, Peter said,

"Ananias, why has Satan filled your heart to lie to the Holy Spirit … you have not lied to men but to God."

The Holy Spirit has a very critical role to play in drawing unsaved people toward God for salvation. First, He protects us from being destroyed by Satan until we decide to accept Jesus Christ (Isaiah 59:19). Second, He convicts us by exposing our sin to us, so we know that we need a Savior (John 16:7–8). Finally, He regenerates us by bringing our spirit to life and giving us a new nature the moment we accept Jesus Christ as Lord and Savior (John 3:3–7; 2 Corinthians 5:17).

After we are saved, and the Holy Spirit resides in us, He begins the life-long work of helping us to live the way God wants us to live. Our bodies become the temple of the Holy Spirit (1 Corinthians 6:19) and He strengthens us for Christian living (Ephesians 3:16). He fills us with His presence if we allow Him the freedom to fill us (Ephesians 5:18). He teaches believers all about spiritual things as we inquire of Him for assistance in understanding God's Word and His ways (John 14:26; 1 John 2:24–27). He gives spiritual gifts to God's children to be used to serve the Body of Christ (1 Corinthians 12:1–11; Ephesians 4:12). He also produces fruit in us that demonstrates our love of God and our transformation from carnal to spiritual (Galatians 5:22–23).

In addition to all the things listed above, the Holy Spirit also performs a life-long process of sanctification by which we are healed and changed from the inside out (Romans 15:16; 2 Thessalonians 2:13). Sanctification requires a separation from the secular and sinful and setting apart for a sacred purpose *(The New Unger's Bible Dictionary)*.

One important thing to know is that the Holy Spirit is a gentleman. He will not force change on you. But if you yield your will to Him and ask Him to help you, the Holy Spirit will expose areas of sin in your life, so you can take those to God and seek His forgiveness, and turn away from that sin and begin living in accordance with God's will for your life. The Holy Spirit lives inside you as a born-again believer, and He has a direct connection to God the Father and God the Son. Isn't that an awesome thought? The Word of God says He intercedes for us. He is your ultimate prayer partner! (Romans 8:26–27).

The Holy Spirit will also reveal areas of deep-rooted pain in your life, which is a result of injuries that you have buried deep within your soul. In order for you to heal from these things, you have to allow Him to show you the root of problem—where it originated. Once the Spirit of God reveals this to you, take that painful incident to Jesus for healing. You may need to forgive someone for hurting you, or take other actions that the Holy Spirit will reveal to you. Sometimes, we bury things so deeply that we don't even recall being hurt because we have blocked it out of our memory. If you want to be healthy physically and spiritually, you can't hold onto the pain you have buried in your soul. It has to be exposed to the light of the truth of God and released to Him for you to obtain complete healing and deliverance.

The Holy Spirit is a powerful advocate and counselor who is standing by to work mightily in your life if you will allow Him to do what He excels at. And that is to help you to turn away from sin in your life, and to heal from past sin and pain that you are holding on to, so you can fully manifest the fruit of the Spirit in your life.

Questions for Reflection:

What have I believed in the past about the Holy Spirit that may be different than what I learned in today's reading?

_____

_____

_____

_____

_____

_____

_____

What should I be more aware of when I think about my body being the Temple of the Holy Spirit that I might not have been aware of before?

_____

_____

_____

_____

_____

_____

_____

Application: Set aside a time of prayer when you focus on allowing the Holy Spirit to intercede for you, allowing Him to pray for you to the Father. Write down any revelations that the Holy Spirit gives to you during this time of prayer.

_____

_____

_____

_____

_____

_____

Prayer: *Thank you, Holy Spirit, for drawing me to Jesus for salvation and for filling me with your power and presence to live the way that God wants me to live. Fill me up and make me more aware of your presence as I seek to draw closer to God each day. Amen.*

My Thoughts/Reflections:

Day 18

LISTENING PRAYER FOR PERSONAL HEALING

The Spirit of the Lord God is upon Me,
Because the Lord has anointed Me
To preach good tidings to the poor;
He has sent Me to heal the brokenhearted,
To proclaim liberty to the captives,
And the opening of the prison to *those who are* bound;

Isaiah 61:1

Prayer is how we communicate with God and one of the most powerful ways that He communicates with us. One form of prayer that has the ability to completely transform your life and deepen your intimacy with the Lord is Listening and Inner Healing Prayer. Jesus came into the world to set us free from sin and the effects of sin in our lives. We read in Luke 4:16–21 that Jesus went into the synagogue in Nazareth and read from the scroll of Isaiah Chapter 61 verse 1, and when He had finished reading the passage, He said, "The Scripture you've just heard has been fulfilled this very day" (Luke 4:21). Jesus was saying that God sent Him to heal our broken hearts, to give liberty to those captive and in bondage to sin, and to open the prisons in our minds that are constructed by Satan to keep us in bondage.

God wants an intimate relationship with you, and He wants to heal all areas of brokenness in your life. He wants you to learn to trust Him and to bring all your cares and concerns to Him in prayer.

Listening prayer is the discipline of sitting quietly before God and allowing Him to speak to you. There is nothing more important for our spiritual growth than being able to discern the voice of God and to allow Him to speak into our lives.

Today let us practice Listening and Inner Healing Prayer. I pray that God will speak healing words to you that will transform your life and ignite a passion in your soul to continue to make Listening prayer a regular practice in your life as you continue to grow spiritually in your relationship with Jesus.

Set aside at least a 30–45 minute block of time and remove all distractions. You may need to go somewhere to get away from your normal surroundings. Have a pen and paper (a prayer journal or a notebook) to write down what God says to you in response to the questions that follow. Prepare your heart and mind to be still before the Lord. After you read each question, write down anything that comes into your mind without trying to analyze it. You may see an image, hear a song, be reminded of a Scripture passage, or just have an impression that something is being said in your heart.

- Jesus, what do you want to say to me?
- Jesus, please search my heart and bring up anything that needs your healing touch.
- Are there any lies that I came to believe as a result of wounding in my past?
- What is the truth? Help me to renounce any lies I have believed.

Questions for Reflection:

What fears or apprehensions did I have about Listening prayer before I tried this exercise?

_____

_____

_____

_____

_____

_____

_____

What can I share with others about this experience that might help them?

_____

_____

_____

_____

_____

_____

_____

_____

Application: Schedule more time for Listening and Inner Healing Prayer over the next several weeks and be sure to journal your experiences, especially writing down what God says to you during these times of prayer.

Prayer: *Lord, help me to set aside times to specifically come to you for inner healing, so you can heal the deep wounds that hinder me from living the abundant life that you promise in Your Word. Amen.*

My Thoughts/Reflections:

Day 19

POWER OF SHARING YOUR TESTIMONY

And they overcame him by the blood of the Lamb and the power of their testimony.

Revelation 12:11

There is great power in the telling and hearing of a personal testimony regarding what God is doing and has done in a person's life. Testimony is defined as a declaration by a witness under oath, as that given before a court or deliberative body; evidence in support of a fact or an assertion; or a public declaration regarding a religious experience *(The American Heritage Dictionary of the English Language)*. The Bible is full of stories about what God did in the lives of His people thousands of years ago. But don't you agree it is a bit hard to relate to some of these stories of people who lived in a far different time, place, and culture than our own?

What if you heard from someone today, who you know and who lives right where you live, about something incredible that God did in his or her life? What if someone you know was healed of an "incurable" disease? Wouldn't that have a stronger impact on you than reading about King Hezekiah being healed from the disease that was supposed to kill him around 700 years before Jesus was born? (Isaiah Chapter 38). What about the testimony of a woman in your town who was barren for years, prayed fervently, and then was able to conceive and have a child? Wouldn't her story have a much more powerful impact on you than reading about Hannah in the Bible who lived approximately 1,000 years before Christ? (1 Samuel Chapter 1). What about hearing the personal testimony of a man or woman who lived for years as a gay man or lesbian, and who, through the power of God working in and through their lives, has walked away from that lifestyle and is now living free from that bondage?

Sharing a personal testimony brings healing and encouragement not only to the person hearing the testimony, but also the person sharing it. For the person sharing, it *seals it* and makes it more real even to them. Sometimes, we can go through something incredible in an almost *out of body* experience where it doesn't become real and tangible to us until we hear ourselves telling the story, or see a video, or hear someone else tell it. Sharing a testimony also reminds the teller of what God did in his or her life, when in the future they may be discouraged about something. Just remembering what God has already done in your life can encourage you to hold on when the going gets rough. If He did it before, He can do it again!

Personal testimonies can move some people toward God like nothing else can. To see living tangible proof of the power of God working in a person's life today might just be the thing that leads someone to Christ. And, by the way, Satan hates it!

Questions for Reflection:

When was the last time I shared my testimony with someone else? What was the impact in that person's life?

_____

_____

_____

_____

_____

_____

_____

If you have never shared your testimony with someone, why?

_____

_____

_____

_____

_____

_____

_____

Application: Write out your testimony using the following format and identify someone to share it with:

How was your life before? What happened?

_____

_____

_____

_____

_____

How did God impact your life for change?

_____

_____

_____

_____

What is different about your life now?

_____

_____

_____

_____

_____

Prayer: *Lord, please open my spiritual eyes to see an opportunity to share my testimony and the courage to do so, that I may bring glory to You through the telling of what you have done in my life. Amen.*

My Thoughts/Reflections:

Day 20

Exposing Pain and Glorifying God

*Confess your trespasses to one another,
and pray for one another, that you may be healed.
The effective, fervent prayer of a righteous man avails much.*

James 5:16

Part of our healing comes from exposing our hurts, pains, and embarrassments instead of burying them. Just like a wound that needs to be opened up and flushed out to purge an infection, wounds that we have experienced in our lives due to things we have done or things that have happened to us need to be opened up and dealt with for complete healing. If we keep these hurts and pains buried, they are buried alive and continue to affect us both physically and spiritually. An important part of our healing process is being able to talk about what we have experienced and how we have been affected by it.

The most effective way to begin healing from your wounds is to spend time in prayer with God, talking to Him about what happened. Like we experience in our times of listening and healing prayer, God will help you to understand how much He loves you, that He was there when you were hurt, and He will help you to heal if you are willing to expose your pains to Him. Just like a child who falls and skins his knee, run to Abba Father and show Him your pain, so He can comfort you and heal your wounds.

Another important way that we obtain healing from the things we have experienced in our lives is to share those experiences and their effect on us with other believers. Spiritual growth is accelerated by our relationships with other Christians. How many times have you been encouraged in your own walk with God when another believer shared with you something they went through, and how God helped them through it? We learn about faith and experience spiritual growth by interacting with other believers.

We read of many instances in the Bible where God enables believers to encourage and be transparent with one another about their real struggles. A few of these passages follow: Hebrews 10:24–25; Matthew 18:20; Romans 7:15–25; and James 5:16. If you hold on to your hurts and are not transparent about your experiences and pains, you are masking the truth and may hinder another person's spiritual growth, in addition to delaying your own healing. It is easy for people who have buried their own pain to believe they are the only ones who have faced what they have experienced. If nobody else is talking about what they have experienced, they may feel all alone in their pain. Once it is exposed to the light, healing begins.

Will you commit to experience healing in some area of your life by exposing an unhealed pain, talking to God about it, and being transparent with another Christian believer about what you have gone through?

Questions for Reflection:

What painful thing(s) have I experienced that I have never shared with anyone before?

_____

_____

_____

_____

_____

_____

_____

_____

Who is God revealing to me that is safe for me to share this with to begin the healing process?

_____

_____

_____

_____

_____

_____

_____

_____

Application: Pray and ask God to reveal to you an area of hurt that has not been dealt with in your life for which He wants you to confess to another believer in Christ for prayer and healing. Prayerfully consider sharing that hurt with the person God reveals to you to share it with.

Prayer: *Lord, my desire is to be free of any buried hurt and pain that hinders my intimacy with You. Help me to be transparent with the right person or persons who can help me to heal and thrive in my relationship with You. Amen.*

My Thoughts/Reflections:

Day 21

IN ALL THINGS PRAISE THE LORD

While I live I will praise the Lord;
I will sing praises to my God while I have my being.

Psalm 146:2

To praise the Lord means *to lift Him up* with our words, to call on Him (2 Samuel 18:28), to recognize His greatness (1 Chronicles 16:25), to recognize His Name (1 Chronicles 29:13), to give credit to His worthiness (Psalm 18:3), to admit proper fear before Him (Psalm 22:23), and to praise His word (Psalm 56:10) *(Holman Treasury of Key Bible Words).*

God inhabits the praises of His people (Psalm 22:3). If you need God's presence close to you today, begin to praise Him! When we praise God, we take the focus off ourselves, and we turn our attention and affections to Him. He loves to inhabit our praises as He loves to have a close abiding relationship with us.

In the Bible, praise was even used as a weapon against the enemy in battle. This seems to be a strange battle plan, but we see in 2 Chronicles 20:21–22 where God defeated the enemies of Jehoshaphat in response to praise. King Jehoshaphat was a God-fearing king who took his concerns to God in prayer and God answered that prayer saying, "Listen, all you of Judah and you inhabitants of Jerusalem, and you, King Jehoshaphat! Thus says the Lord to you: 'Do not be afraid nor dismayed because of this great multitude, for the battle *is* not yours, but God's'" (2 Chronicles 20:15). Read the whole story in 2 Chronicles Chapter 20; it is amazing!

Various methods of praise are found in the Bible, including kneeling down or bowing (Psalm 95:6), lifting hands in praise (2 Chronicles 6:12), praising God with singing and instrumental music (Psalm 33:1–3), dancing before the Lord (2 Samuel 6:14), and shouting joyfully to the Lord (Psalm 98:4–9). The most important thing about praise is not necessarily how you do it, but that your heart is in a posture of praise.

We are to praise God all day long. From the rising of the sun to its setting, the Lord's name is to be praised (Psalm 113:3). Make praise a regular part of your worship of God every day.

Questions for Reflection:

When was the last time I truly praised the Lord?

_____

_____

_____

_____

_____

_____

_____

How would my prayer life and my faith be transformed if I praised the Lord every day?

_____

_____

_____

_____

_____

_____

_____

_____

Application: Try praising God in a way that you have never expressed before, based on the biblical examples of praise in this devotion.

Prayer: *Lord, my desire is to praise You from the sun's rising to its setting! Help me to overcome any fear, apprehension, or distraction that may hinder my praise, so it is a blessing to You. Amen.*

My Thoughts/Reflections:

Day 22

SHARING WHAT GOD HAS DONE FOR YOU WITH OTHERS

*To the weak I became as weak,
that I might win the weak.
I have become all things to all men,
that I might by all means save some.*

1 Corinthians 9:22

God uses people and their stories to draw others to Him. Think about it. Has anyone in your life ever shared his or her faith with you? If you are like most people, you heard the Gospel message more than once from several different people before you responded to and accepted Jesus Christ.

In addition to drawing people to the saving knowledge of Jesus Christ through the sharing of the Gospel, God uses the stories of His impact on ordinary everyday people to give others hope, to increase their faith, and to bring them comfort. When we hear about what God miraculously did for someone else when we are in the midst of a struggle or in the midst of pain and suffering, it may be just what we need to hold on a little longer and to actually believe it could happen for us, too!

God is working in the lives of his children—all of us—including you. He does not want you to keep to yourself what He has done in your life. He wants you to share it with others. He loves to hear His children talking about what an incredible God He is and what He has done for them. Think about how good it feels to hear someone talking to someone else about what a good friend you are, or what a good parent you are, and what great things you have done for them.

When we share what God has done in our lives, we need to tailor the message to the listener. Now, the story of what God did for you doesn't change, but in order to communicate it well, you need to modify how you deliver the message, so it comes across in the most powerful and effective way to various audiences.

Here is an example. When sharing your salvation testimony with someone who has never been in a church before, it would be ineffective to use "church" words like salvation, saved, blood of the Lamb, and so on because he or she will not know what you are talking about and may think you are a little strange. It is much more effective to simply tell the story using everyday words they can understand: "I used to live a self-centered life. I was never satisfied and always wondered why I was even here. I discovered that I was a sinner and that my sins were separating me from God. That is when I met Jesus. He died to take away my sins and to restore my relationship with God. I asked Jesus for forgiveness, and He restored me to God, and my whole life has changed! I now have a peace that I never knew before." You get the idea.

We also need to be careful to tailor our testimony to listeners based on their age, maturity level, and so on. This is especially important when sharing your deliverance testimony. Only include the details that are appropriate for the listener. The Apostle Paul shared his testimony several different ways based on the audience before him each time. Read the following instances where Paul's story is recounted to see how the story was tailored based on the audience:

- Acts 9:1–3 (Luke's account of Paul's conversion)
- Acts 21:37 thru Acts 22:22 (Paul speaking to a mob in Jerusalem)
- Acts 26:1–29 (Paul speaking to King Agrippa)
- 1 Corinthians 15:1–11 (Paul writing to the Corinthian church)
- Galatians 1:11–24 (Paul writing to the Galatian church)

Questions for Reflection:

What was the core of the message that Paul shared with each audience?

_____

_____

_____

_____

_____

_____

_____

Why did he tell it differently to different audiences?

_____

_____

_____

_____

_____

_____

_____

Application: Identify three different audiences or people who would benefit from hearing your story and make notes regarding what changes would be necessary to effectively communicate your message to each group while keeping the core of the message the same.

_____

_____

_____

_____

_____

_____

_____

_____

Prayer: *Lord, please sensitize me to the slight delivery modifications that I should make to my testimony story to have the maximum impact on those who hear my message, so You are glorified and my story makes a positive impact in their lives. Amen.*

My Thoughts/Reflections:

Day 23

WITNESSING: THE GREAT COMMISSION

*Go therefore and make disciples of all the nations,
baptizing them in the name of the Father
and of the Son and of the Holy Spirit,
teaching them to observe all things
that I have commanded you; and lo, I am with you always,
even to the end of the age. Amen.*

Matthew 28:19–20

After Jesus was raised from the dead and appeared to his disciples, He commissioned them to make disciples of all the nations. He told them to baptize believers in the name of the Father and of the Son and of the Holy Spirit, teaching believers to observe all the things He had commanded them.

Jesus also calls us to make disciples by sharing the great news of the Gospel with unbelievers.

Every believer is commanded by Jesus to share the Gospel with unbelievers (Matthew 28:19; Mark 16:15; Luke 24:47; John 20:21). This is not just a job for pastors and ministers. All of us are to share the Gospel as well, and the Holy Spirit will enable you to share it with His power (Acts 1:8).

Do you remember who led you to Christ? Perhaps you heard a sermon or read a book that pricked your heart, or maybe someone shared the Good News with you one-on-one. One way to lead a person to Christ is to follow a series of Scriptures known as the *Romans Road to Salvation*. The book of Romans lays out the Gospel message in an easy to understand story.

The Romans Road story begins by revealing the current state of the unsaved. We are all born into sin as a result of Adam and Eve's Fall in the Garden of Eden. The story goes on to demonstrate the amazing love of Jesus Christ for all of man: while we were still living in sin, Jesus Christ died on the cross to take away the sins of the world.

The only requirement for man to be saved is to accept the free gift of salvation offered by God. There is absolutely nothing we can do to earn a right to be called a child of God and to earn salvation and eternal life. This is a free gift offered by God to any person who recognizes the sacrificial death of Jesus, and who believes by faith alone that Jesus died for him or her. When that person calls on the name of the Lord Jesus Christ, he or she WILL be saved.

This is the great news of the Gospel. Every child of God is commanded to share this Good News with others. The Romans Road to Salvation story follows this order of Scriptures:

- Romans 3:10
- Romans 3:23
- Romans 5:12
- Romans 5:8
- Romans 6:23
- Romans 10:9–10
- Romans 10:13

As the Great Commission instructs us, we should always be ready to share the Gospel message with unbelievers. Whether you use Romans Road or another method to communicate the Gospel message, be ready to share the hope that is within you to those you come into contact with each day.

Questions for Reflection:

When was the last time I shared the Gospel message with someone who did not know about the gift of salvation offered to them by Jesus?

_____

_____

_____

_____

_____

_____

_____

_____

If you do not regularly share your faith with others, what is hindering you?

_____

_____

_____

_____

_____

_____

_____

_____

Application: Look for opportunities to share your faith with unbelievers and step out on faith that God will open doors for you if you are willing to be vulnerable and bold for Him. Know that He is with you and will help you to draw others to Him.

Prayer: *Lord, help me to overcome any fears I may have about sharing the Gospel message with others and give me a boldness to obey the Great Commission as it applies to me. Amen.*

My Thoughts/Reflections:

Day 24

WHAT IS FAITH?

*Now faith is the substance of things hoped for,
the evidence of things not seen.*

Hebrews 11:1

Faith is a term difficult to define or explain. Faith is easier to understand through examples of people who have demonstrated it. Hebrews Chapter 11 recounts stories of the lives of many people who demonstrated faith through their actions. Here we learn of the faith of Abraham who obeyed God when he was called to leave behind everything he knew and go where God directed him and do what God asked of him. As a result, he is referred to as the father of our faith (Romans 4:16).

By faith, the walls of Jericho fell down after they were encircled for seven days (Hebrews 11:30; Joshua 6:1–20). This was a demonstration of faith by a whole group of people that resulted in the miraculous defeat of a fortified city. By faith, Moses led the Israelite slaves out of Egypt, the land of their bondage. They even walked through the midst of the Red Sea on dry ground in the miraculous Exodus from Egypt (Hebrews 11:29; Exodus 14:1–31). Through Moses' faith, the people came to believe in the saving power of the LORD.

In the New Testament, we learn that a centurion (a Roman army officer) sent Jewish elders to Jesus to plead with Him to heal his very sick servant who was dear to him and near death. The centurion asked that Jesus just say a word to heal his servant, and Jesus responded by saying to the crowd that followed Him, "I say to you, I have not found such great faith, not even in Israel" (Luke 7:9). Here we see that the centurion had great faith in the healing power and authority of Jesus. He placed his faith and trust in Jesus and his servant was healed just as he had asked.

Elsewhere in the Bible, we learn of a group of four friends who pursued Jesus on behalf of their paralyzed friend. They carried their friend to the roof above where Jesus was teaching and broke through the roof to lower the man down in front of Him. When Jesus saw their faith, He said to the paralytic, "Son, your sins are forgiven you" (Mark 2:5). He then healed the man who was then able to walk out carrying his mat (Mark 2:1–12). Once again, we see the faith of a group of people. It was their faith that moved Jesus to heal the paralytic.

Faith is closely tied to belief, and the essence of faith is trust. Faith is the substance of things hoped for. It is the *stuff* of what we hope for. When we act on our faith—like Abraham, Moses, the centurion, and all the others—it is a demonstration or evidence of things not seen. Abraham did not see the Promised Land, yet he obeyed God to begin the journey toward it. Moses had to step into the water of the Red Sea before it opened up before him. The centurion had to send for Jesus and ask him to speak a word to heal his servant before he saw the result. We too must exercise our faith, for we are all sons and daughters of God through faith in Christ Jesus (Galatians 4:26).

Finally, the Bible says that without faith, it is impossible to please Him, for he who comes to God must believe that He is, and that He is a rewarder of those who diligently seek Him (Hebrews 11:6). Let us diligently seek the Lord and exercise our faith today.

Questions for Reflection:

When was the last time I exercised my faith in the Lord? Trusting in Him for something that I could not see ahead of time?

_____

_____

_____

_____

_____

_____

_____

Who helped me come to faith in Jesus Christ?

_____

_____

_____

_____

_____

_____

_____

Application: Think of someone in your life who could benefit from hearing how God responded to your faith and then find an opportunity to share the story with that person.

Prayer: *Lord, increase my faith. Help me to live out my faith and to share my faith with others who need to know that You can be trusted with their lives. Amen.*

My Thoughts/Reflections:

Day 25

TRUST IN THE LORD

Trust in the Lord with all your heart,
And lean not on your own understanding;
In all your ways acknowledge Him,
And He shall direct your paths.

Proverbs 3:5–6

Who do you trust? Have you ever trusted someone, only to be disappointed by that person? Only the Lord God is completely trustworthy. Abram and Sarai learned a powerful lesson about trusting God. In Genesis Chapter 18, the Lord appeared to them and said they would have a son to fulfill God's earlier promise to Abraham that he would father a child, and that his descendants would outnumber the stars, and that he would be the father of many nations (Genesis 15:4–5; 17:5). The apparent problem with this promise was that both of them were old by this time, and she was well past the normal age of childbearing. But is anything too difficult for the LORD? (Genesis 18:14).

Years passed and this promised child did not come as expected by Abram and Sarai, so she devised a plan to have her Egyptian maidservant Hagar sleep with her husband to bear a child for him. Sarai was not trusting God to come through on His promise to them. As soon as Ishmael was born, she despised her maidservant and there was trouble in the family. Years later, when Abram was ninety-nine years old, God appeared to him again, changed his name to Abraham, Sarai's name to Sarah, and restated the promise that she would bear the child of promise. Abraham was one hundred years old and Sarah ninety when their son Isaac was born! The time between the original promise from God to Abram of a son to carry on his legacy and the birth of Isaac was 25 years.

In this story, we see what happened when Sarai and Abram leaned to their own understanding, trying to figure out a way to have a child they could call their own when this promise from God was not being fulfilled as quickly as they would have liked. They were getting older, year by year, and not seeing how this was going to be possible. But God is faithful and trustworthy, and He will fulfill His promises on His timeline.

When we turn to our own understanding and do not acknowledge God, we end up traveling on our own path. But if we lean on Him, trust Him completely, and wait on the Lord, He will direct our path and fulfill His plans and purposes for our lives.

Questions for Reflection:

What promise(s) has God made to me that I have yet to see fulfilled?

_____

_____

_____

_____

_____

_____

_____

Am I willing to wait as long as it takes, or have I made the mistake of trying to hurry the process?

_____

_____

_____

_____

_____

_____

_____

_____

Application: Write a prayer to God affirming your trust in Him alone. You can write out Proverbs 3:5–7, making it your personal prayer.

_____

_____

_____

_____

_____

_____

_____

Prayer: *Lord, I confess that I have not trusted You with my whole heart and have leaned to my own understanding in some areas of my life. My desire is to allow You alone to direct my paths and to fulfill Your plans for my life, in Jesus name I pray. Amen.*

My Thoughts/Reflections:

Day 26

FEAR OF THE LORD

The fear of the Lord is the beginning of wisdom,
And the knowledge of the Holy One is understanding.

Proverbs 9:10

We do not hear much today about the fear of the Lord. In an era of hyper-grace, people want to believe that God is gracious, loving and kind, and that He *looks the other way* when we *mess up* and forgives us when we *miss the mark*. Yes—He is gracious, loving and kind, but He is also Holy and righteous, and He is a fearsome Judge who does not tolerate sin. But in accordance with your hardness and your impenitent heart, you are treasuring up for yourself wrath in the day of wrath and revelation of the righteous judgment of God, who "will render to each one according to his deeds": eternal life to those who by patient continuance in doing good seek for glory, honor, and immortality; but to those who are self-seeking and do not obey the truth, but obey unrighteousness—indignation and wrath, tribulation and anguish, on every soul of man who does evil (Romans 5:5–8). Thankfully, Jesus took the punishment that we deserve for our sins when He died on the cross, was buried, and rose again! His free gift of salvation is available to all who believe by faith that He did this for them.

God performed fearsome acts of judgment upon Egypt and its false gods when Pharaoh refused to release the Israelite slaves from bondage. He turned water into blood, sent frogs, lice, wild animals, locusts, hail and fire, and caused disease in livestock and boils on man and beast. He caused deep darkness to fall on the land for three days and finally caused the death of all the firstborn of Egypt. When Israel saw the great power, which the LORD had used against the Egyptians, the people feared the LORD, and they believed in the LORD and in His servant Moses (Exodus 14:31). These judgments caused the Israelites to revere God.

Another type of fear of the Lord that we see in Scripture is the fear that keeps a person from sinning because he or she loves God and wants to please Him. He who walks in his uprightness fears the Lord, but he who is perverse in his ways despises Him (Proverbs 14:2). This fear dreads God's displeasure, desires His favor, reveres His holiness, submits cheerfully to His will, is grateful for His benefits, sincerely worships Him, and conscientiously obeys His commandments *(The New Unger's Bible Dictionary)*.

Knowledge of the Holy One is understanding. "Because they hated knowledge and did not choose the fear of the Lord, they would have none of my counsel and despised my every rebuke. Therefore, they shall eat the fruit of their own way, and be filled to the full with their own fancies. For the turning away of the simple will slay them, and the complacency of fools will destroy them but whoever listens to me will dwell safely, and will be secure, without fear of evil" (Proverbs 1:29–33). Only when we truly understand God as the Holy One and fear Him do we have understanding.

Questions for Reflection:

In what ways have I misunderstood the fear of the Lord?

How has the fear of the Lord kept me from sinning?

Application: Think of a time when you feared man more than God in something you did, said, or failed to do, and you asked God for forgiveness.

Prayer: *Lord, forgive me for losing sight of Your Holiness. I desire to worship You with my life, always walking uprightly before You. Keep my perspective in check, and do not allow me to be drawn into a hyper-grace understanding of who You are. Amen.*

My Thoughts/Reflections:

Day 27
ABIDING IN CHRIST

*Abide in Me, and I in you. As the branch cannot
bear fruit of itself, unless it abides in the vine,
neither can you, unless you abide in Me.*

John 15:4

To abide means to remain or stay. In the above passage, Jesus commands us to abide in Him. It is not a suggestion; it is a command. We are commanded to remain *in* Him. Think of an apple tree. Does the branch of an apple tree have to work to produce an apple? No—the branch has only to remain attached firmly to the trunk of the tree to draw nourishment from the soil in which it is planted and to absorb the light from the sun through its leaves. The apple is produced as a result of the work that God does in that tree to bring forth its fruit. If the branch is broken away from the trunk of the tree, no fruit can be produced by that branch. It withers and dies. This is exactly what happens to us spiritually if we become disconnected from Jesus through unrepentant sin or by letting the cares of the world override our devotion to God.

All we have to do is abide in Jesus and God does the work in us to bring forth new life and keep us spiritually healthy. What does this look like? To abide in Jesus, we have to be aligned with Him and develop a personal relationship with Him. This includes spending time in His Word, obeying what He commands, and expressing our love and devotion to Him through prayer, praise and worship.

Jesus goes on to say in John 15:5 that "I am the vine, you are the branches. He who abides in Me, and I in him, bears much fruit;

for without Me you can do nothing." Notice that He says if we abide in Him, we bring forth *much* fruit.

The fruit of the Spirit is love, joy, peace, longsuffering, kindness, goodness, faithfulness, gentleness and self-control (Galatians 5:22–23). The fruit that we can expect as a result of abiding in Christ will transform our lives as it changes us into His image. He will radically re-orient our lives, altering the whole "fabric of our being" to include our thinking, feeling, willing and acting.

Imagine how your life would be transformed if you had an abundant expression of every fruit of the Spirit fully operating in your life! Jesus tells us the way: Abide in Him.

Questions for Reflection:

How would I rate my current level of abiding in the Lord?

_____

_____

_____

_____

_____

_____

_____

_____

What fruit is evident in my life as a result of abiding in Jesus?

_____

_____

_____

_____

_____

_____

_____

_____

Application: Examine your current relationship with Jesus and ask Him to show you how you can deepen your relationship with Him and increase your spiritual fruit.

Prayer: *Lord, thank you for your desire to abide in me. Help me to align my life to abide in You more fully, totally surrendering my will to You, so you can produce in me a great harvest of the fruit of the Spirit. Amen.*

My Thoughts/Reflections:

Day 28

SANCTIFICATION: A LIFE-LONG PROCESS

*But we all, with unveiled face, beholding as in a mirror
the glory of the Lord, are being transformed into
the same image from glory to glory,
just as by the Spirit of the Lord.*

2 Corinthians 3:18

Sanctification is defined as the process of becoming consecrated to God *(The Dictionary of Bible Themes)*. It is a life-long process whereby we are separated from sin and dedicated to God for His use. Sanctification begins in believers' hearts and frees them from the power of sin. It is a progressive work of the Holy Spirit who makes believers more and more like Jesus as they are changed into His image over their lifetime.

It is God's will that we be and live holy by the sacrifice of the body of Jesus Christ. We have been sanctified through the offering of the body of Jesus Christ once for all (Hebrews 10:10). Jesus died for our sins so those who believe are no longer controlled by sin but by the Spirit of God who dwells within them. For sin shall not have dominion over you, for you are not under law but under grace (Romans 6:14).

We are sanctified by the Word of God, self-examination, prayer and obedience. We cannot continue to view sin the same way we did before we were regenerated. Therefore, if anyone is in Christ, he is a new creation; old things have passed away; behold, all things have become new (2 Corinthians 5:17). As a new creation in Christ, we have to diligently focus on our new life in Christ and not allow ourselves to slide back into old familiar sinful habits.

The power of the Holy Spirit (in our new spiritual life) keeps us from yielding to a life of sin. The Apostle Paul writes to the church in Corinth that it should not be deceived because people who persist in sin will not inherit the Kingdom of God. He then goes on to encourage the church by saying, "And such were some of you. But you were washed, but you were sanctified, but you were justified in the name of the Lord Jesus and by the Spirit of our God" (1 Corinthians 6:11).

Sanctification that transforms us into the image of Christ requires surrender on our part. We cannot maintain control of our lives and expect the Holy Spirit to force transformation on us. We must surrender daily to the work of the Spirit in our lives as we seek to live a holy life that is pleasing to God.

We must abide in Christ and look into the mirror of the Word of God and examine our own lives to see if we are aligned with His Word. Then we must be obedient to what God reveals to us through His Word and prayer. "But be doers of the word, and not hearers only, deceiving yourselves. For if anyone is a hearer of the word and not a doer, he is like a man observing his natural face in a mirror; for he observes himself, goes away, and immediately forgets what kind of man he was. But he who looks into the perfect law of liberty and continues in it, and is not a forgetful hearer but a doer of the work, this one will be blessed in what he does" (James 1:22–25).

Questions for Reflection:

How has my life been transformed since I first surrendered my life to Jesus?

_____

_____

_____

_____

_____

_____

_____

Think back over the past year. How would you evaluate your progression in sanctification?

_____

_____

_____

_____

_____

_____

_____

_____

Application: Examine your life to determine what needs to change in order to allow the Holy Spirit to continue or increase the rate of your sanctification. Do you need to spend more time in His Word? Do you need to surrender to the work of the Spirit? Do you need to obey what He has already told you?

Prayer: *Lord, thank you for the sacrificial death of Jesus Christ on the cross for my sins and for beginning the sanctification process in my life. Help me to surrender completely to the work of the Holy Spirit who is transforming me into Your image day by day. Amen.*

My Thoughts/Reflections:

Day 29

SPIRITUAL GIFTS AND CALLING

*As each one has received a gift,
minister it to one another,
as good stewards of the manifold grace of God.*

1 Peter 4:10

A variety of Spiritual Gifts are listed in the Bible. Some are considered supernatural manifestations of the Holy Spirit's work through a believer. Others are motivational gifts, and still others are considered ministry gifts. Regardless of what you call them or how they are displayed in a believer's life, they are all given to us by God and are to be used in service to other people and to bring glory and honor to the One who gave them to us.

The Church is sometimes described in terms of the people who make up the various parts of the Body. (See 1 Corinthians Chapter 12). Each person in the Body of Christ has a role to play using the gifts that God has equipped him or her with. No one gift is more important than any other. Just as every part of the physical body is important, the Church Body doesn't function well when a part is missing or not operating to its full potential. The Body of Christ needs each and every member operating in the gift given by God to be healthy and whole.

Spiritual Gifts Scriptures:

- Manifestation Gifts (1 Corinthians 12:1–11)
- Motivational Gifts (Romans 12:3–8)
- Ministry Gifts (Ephesians 4:7–16)

To learn which Spiritual Gifts you have been given and how you can use them to serve others, you can take a Spiritual Gifts survey. Such an instrument can be found in books and pamphlets in Christian bookstores. Free online Spiritual Gifts inventories are also available. Try https://gifts.churchgrowth.org/spiritual-gifts-survey/ or search online for "Spiritual Gifts Inventory."

If you are not already using your Spiritual Gifts in service to the Body of Christ, make a commitment to learn more about your gifts and how to use them as God intended. You will be blessed when you are operating in the center of God's will—and that includes operating and functioning in the unique gifting that has been given to you in service to others.

Questions for Reflection:

Have I been using my Spiritual Gifts in service to the Body of Christ? Why or Why not?

_____

_____

_____

_____

_____

_____

_____

Which distinctive giftings has God given me that only I can put into service in a unique way to benefit others?

_____

_____

_____

_____

_____

_____

_____

_____

Application: Discover and learn as much as you can about the unique gifts God has given you to serve the Body of Christ, and then make a commitment to serve others using your gifts.

Prayer: *Lord, help me to understand the unique calling you have on my life to serve others with the gifts you have given me to build up the Body of Christ. Give me a desire to use these gifts to their fullest potential to bring glory and honor to You. Amen.*

My Thoughts/Reflections:

Day 30

Your Life's Purpose

*For we are His workmanship, created in Christ Jesus
for good works, which God prepared beforehand
that we should walk in them.*

Ephesians 2:10

God has a plan and a purpose for your life. In addition to your deliverance and healing from the wounds associated with personal bondage to sin, God wants to use you and your testimony to bring other people to the saving knowledge of Him. He created you, loves you, and has been preparing you for your Mission your whole life (Ephesians 2:10).

Just like Paul and many others in the Bible, God will use the story of your life to bring glory and honor to Him as you are obedient to do what He reveals to you. When we look outside our own lives and see our circumstances from God's eye view, we can see that He has been preparing us all our lives to come to know and serve Him. Isaiah 55:8–9 says, "'For My thoughts are not your thoughts, nor are your ways My ways,' says the Lord. 'For as the heavens are higher than the earth, so are My ways higher than your ways, and My thoughts than your thoughts.'" God sees the big picture and knows exactly how He wants you to serve Him.

Today, you will begin to draft your personal Mission and Vision Statements. There is power in writing down what God reveals to you. Just like the power of the written Word in the Bible, writing down the truth that God reveals to you as you pray and ask Him to show you how He wants to use your life is the first step to seeing those plans displayed in your life.

Writing and continuously reviewing your personal Mission and Vision statements also helps you to stay focused on the things that God has uniquely gifted and equipped you to contribute as part of the Body of Christ. There are numerous 'good things' that you can be doing, but if they distract from the Mission and Vision that God has revealed, you will be less effective and may get burned out. After you have your clear Mission and Vision from God, evaluate every opportunity that comes your way and see if it will advance or detract from what He has assigned you to do. Only participate in activities that move you closer to your Mission and Vision.

Please know that we are not saved by the works that we do for God. For by grace you have been saved through faith, and that not of yourselves; it is the gift of God, not of works, lest anyone should boast (Ephesians 2:8–9). Our salvation comes from the finished work of Jesus Christ and our faith in Him alone. The works that we do are a natural response to the amazing gift of salvation given to us by Jesus Christ, and the Word tells us that our faith without works is dead (James 2:14–26).

Steps to developing a personal Mission and Vision Statement:

- Take some time to pray and ask God to begin to speak to you about your future, writing down what He is showing you, as well as any associated Scripture references He brings to mind.
- Think of your Spiritual Gifts as well as the other gifts He has bestowed on you (e.g., material, physical, time, talents, etc.). Write down the gifts that God has given you and wants you to use to bring glory and honor to Him.
- Pray and ask God to reveal to you the Vision He has for your life—what He desires to see manifest in your life as a result of what He has done for you. This is a forward-looking statement that is not attainable yet. It

is the desired result of your obedience to use what God has gifted you to advance His Kingdom here on earth.

- Pray and ask God to reveal to you the specific Mission He has for you to attain the Vision He has revealed to you. This too is a forward-looking statement. A Mission Statement essentially answers the question "How will I attain my Vision?"

I will share with you my Vision and Mission statements as an example:

Vision: To see people delivered and healed from the bondage of sin through an intimate, personal relationship with Jesus Christ.

> *Scripture Reference:* Therefore, if anyone is in Christ, he is a new creation; old things have passed away; behold, all things have become new (2 Corinthians 5:17).

Mission: To draw unrepentant sinners and lukewarm Christians into an intimate life-transforming relationship with Jesus Christ by sharing my testimony and proclaiming the Gospel.

> *Scripture Reference:* And the Lord said, "(Debora, Debora!) Indeed, Satan has asked for you, that he may sift you as wheat. But I have prayed for you, that your faith should not fail; and when you have returned to Me, strengthen your brethren" (Luke 22:31–32).

I challenge you to take all the time that is needed to develop personal Mission and Vision statements and to display them prominently where you will be constantly reminded of what God has uniquely gifted you and charged you to accomplish for Him. Review them and revise them as needed as you grow in the gifts and calling that God has assigned you.

Questions for Reflection:

What is my personal Vision Statement?

_____
_____
_____
_____
_____
_____
_____
_____

What is my personal Mission Statement?

_____
_____
_____
_____
_____
_____
_____
_____

Application: After writing down your personal Vision and Mission statements, create a visible reminder to display these statements prominently, so they can be seen daily. This can be a poster, painting, calligraphy, framed print, bookmark, or any other creative way to display these, so you are constantly reminded of the Vision and Mission God has assigned you.

Prayer: *Lord, help me to fulfill the plans and purposes that you have for my life. Guide me to define my personal Vision and Mission statements, so I can focus my efforts and resources on the things that matter to You. Amen.*

My Thoughts/Reflections:

Day 31

Continuing Intimacy with Jesus

*Your word is a lamp to my feet
And a light to my path.*

Psalm 119:105

You have been on quite a journey! Look at how far you have come in your spiritual growth and in your healing from the effects of sinful behaviors and the development of a deeper intimacy with Jesus. This is just the beginning of the rest of your life, and I know that God has a great plan and purpose for your life.

You have been disciplined in studying the Word of God by completing the reflection questions and application exercises. Now, it is time for you to develop your own plan to continue abiding in Jesus Christ and His Word for continual growth and healing. God's Word is powerful, and it heals and changes lives. For the Word of God is living and powerful, and sharper than any two-edged sword, piercing even to the division of soul and spirit, joints and marrow, and is a discerner of the thoughts and intents of the heart (Hebrews 4:12).

You may want to go back to Day 1 and work slowly through this devotional, taking more than a single day to review each devotional lesson until you get everything possible out of them. Continual spiritual growth requires discipline. God wants to maintain an intimate and personal relationship with you. He has so much more for your life, and in order for Him to continue to heal your wounds and produce fruit in your life, you have to continue to abide in Him. Jesus says, "Abide in Me, and I in you. As the branch cannot bear fruit of itself, unless it abides in the vine, neither can you, unless you abide in Me" (John 15:4). He also promises that if you abide in His Word and meditate on what it teaches, you will be rooted, productive to the Kingdom of God, and prosperous. "He shall be like a tree planted by the rivers of water, that brings forth its fruit in its season, whose leaf also shall not wither; and whatever he does shall prosper" (Psalm 1:3).

God will continue to transform your life as He sanctifies you day by day if you remain in His Word and stay connected to Jesus and to other believers. No matter how far you have come over the course of this study or how far you have yet to go in your healing from the effects of your bondage to sin, the Word of God promises change and newness in your life. "Therefore, if anyone is in Christ, he is a new creation; old things have passed away; behold, all things have become new" (2 Corinthians 5:17). Walk in the newness of your life in Christ.

May God bless you as you continue your intimate walk with Him. I pray that "He would grant you, according to the riches of His glory, to be strengthened with might through His Spirit in the inner man, that Christ may dwell in your hearts through faith; that you, being rooted and grounded in love, may be able to comprehend with all the saints what is the width and length and depth and height—to know the love of Christ which passes knowledge; that you may be filled with all the fullness of God" (Ephesians 3:16–19).

Questions for Reflection:

What is my plan to continue to abide in the Word and apply what I have learned during the course of this study to my life?

_____

_____

_____

_____

_____

_____

_____

Who can I share this material with and invite to walk with me through this devotional again to get even more out of the lessons it contains?

_____

_____

_____

_____

_____

_____

_____

Application: Prayerfully consider slowly repeating each devotional lesson, taking as much time as is necessary to get the most out of each lesson. Invite others to go through the lessons with you, so you can share with one another what you are learning.

Prayer: *Thank you, Lord, for all that you have revealed to me as I have spent time working through this devotional. Continue to challenge me to confess my sins to you and to diligently study Your Word and spend quality time with You every day. Amen.*

My Thoughts/Reflections:

About the Author

Debora is an ordained minister, author, and speaker whose life has been completely transformed by the unconditional love of Jesus Christ! She lived many years in rebellion to God, openly denying His existence, and living a life centered around her own ways of thinking and her own desires to please herself. But God had a greater purpose and plan for her life, and He relentlessly pursued her even when she was denying His existence.

Debora surrendered her life to Jesus and started reading and applying the Word of God to her life. The Bible so powerfully transformed her life, that she is an entirely new creation. Her purpose in life is to share what she has learned with others, so they too can experience the life-transforming grace and power of Jesus Christ!

Therefore, if anyone is in Christ, he is a new creation; old things have passed away; behold, all things have become new (2 Corinthians 5:17 NKJV).

Debora Barr
www.allthingsnewlifetransformation.org
www.dbarrministries.org
DBarrMinistries@gmail.com

www.ingramcontent.com/pod-product-compliance
Lightning Source LLC
Chambersburg PA
CBHW060537100426
42743CB00009B/1551